Decluttering Made Easy: How to Declutter Your Home on a Dime

By Juliana Yates

Free Bonus: Download our FREE Holiday Gift Guide at the link below:

http://holidaygiftnation.com/gift-guide/

Author Introduction

I am Juliana Yates, and years ago I became fed up with the clutter in my household. Between children, pets, myself, and my partner, there was a never ending flow of "stuff" flowing into, but not out of my house. That is NOT a sustainable situation, so I finally decided to do something about it. Decluttering not only makes your house look better, but it also clears your mind. When you live in a cluttered space, your mind cannot help but be cluttered as well.

Of course, I did not have the money to hire a professional organizer for my household, so I had to figure out how to declutter on a dime. There is never a bad time to save money, but today's economic times make frugality something families and individuals of all situations are striving to achieve. With pay cuts, job losses, and the ever-rising prices of things like milk, meat, and produce, saving money throughout the home helps to maintain a better quality of life even in hard economic times. One way you can enhance that quality of life and save money is through decluttering and organizing your home.

I am sharing my very best decluttering tips, tricks, how-tos, and what-not-to-dos in this eBook. Read it today, start decluttering, and enjoy a happier, less stressful lifestyle almost immediately. You will be happy that you took the time to read my book and declutter your home and life!

Contents

Author Introduction 3

How Decluttering Your Home Improves Quality of Life 6

How to Save Money Decluttering Your Home 7

Five Common Organizational and Decluttering Mistakes 10

Reducing Clutter 12

Classify everything. 12

Take Action 14

Use Frugal Organization Tips to Design a New Space 15

Organizing in a Frugal Fashion 16

Shop Dollar Stores for Storage Bargains 16

Shop Outside the Storage Aisle 18

Shop Used and Online 21

Use What You Already Have 22

Organization for Your Entire Home: Decluttering Five Main Areas 23

Tips for Decluttering the Kitchen 23

Tips for Decluttering the Living room 25

Tips for Decluttering Bedrooms 27

Tips for Decluttering the Bathroom 30

Tips for Decluttering the Home Office 32

Declutter as a Family 34

Decluttering Childrens' Incoming Paper 35

Conclusion: Anyone Can Live Clutter-Free 36

More Home & Health Resource Guides 37

How Decluttering Your Home Improves Quality of Life

You may not realize how much your stuff controls your life. Disorganization and clutter can make it hard to find things you want, get in the way of the maintenance of your home, and cause additional stress in your life. Among the many ways that too much or unorganized stuff can cost you time and money include:

- o Making you late for work or other commitments because you can't find keys, articles of clothing, or materials necessary for your job or school.
- o Causing you to spend additional funds to purchase duplicate items that you can't locate at home.
- o Increasing grocery bills unnecessarily because you don't have a good understanding of what is in your pantry.
- o Increasing maintenance or repair costs due to the fact that unorganized items are more likely to suffer damage.

Removing clutter reduces the stress of stuff, allows you to open your home to friends and family at any time without feeling like you need to conduct over-the-top spring cleaning, and keeps your belongings safe and secure.

How to Save Money Decluttering Your Home

Many times people avoid decluttering and organizing their homes because they feel like they don't have the time or money to spend on the endeavor. If you pass through the organizational aisle of any home improvement or department store, you can see why people think it will be an expensive undertaking. A small specialty shelf in a discount department store can run $50 and the same type of item can cost over $200 in a home décor boutique.

The good news is, you don't have to limit yourself to these types of items. By employing some of the tips and tricks I outline in the following chapters throughout your home, you can cut organizational costs by over 75 percent while maintaining a beautiful and uncluttered area that you can still live in.

Decluttering to Help Save or Make Money

One of the aspects of decluttering you may find is that it can help you save or even make money. For example, you can gather up old items that are simply sitting around in the basement, attic, or any other room, and sell them on the eBay auction site, where avid buyers of all sorts of items search daily. Additionally, you can make it easier with less worry about shipping by selling locally in a community yard sale, your own garage sale, or by placing a listing on the Craigslist site.

To place ads on eBay, you'll need to sign up for a membership. There are also fees involved based on the price you list your item at to start with, whether or not you offer a "Buy it Now" price, and based on your final sales price.

With Craigslist, there normally is not a fee involved, but you will need to sign up for a free account to create ads. You can list your items in a few local towns or cities you are in or nearby for maximum exposure. Always be careful about the people you arrange to meet on Craigslist. Use common sense safety measures with people you do not know.

With both eBay and Craigslist, the key will be writing great descriptions and including at least a few pictures of the item so buyers will know exactly what they are getting. Doing these simple things could mean earning some great extra money for those items you have just laying around.

The other aspect to think about is donating items to a local church, community center, or places such as the Salvation Army or Goodwill. The way this helps save money is because you can use the donation as a tax deduction, which may mean paying less on your income tax return, or possibly getting more back!

It's important to always keep these ideas in mind when you're considering just "throwing stuff away." Remember the popular phrase, "One person's trash, is another's treasure!"

Five Common Organizational and Decluttering Mistakes

Before we take a look at things you should do to organize your home on a budget, let's look at five of the most common mistakes people make when they declutter their home. These mistakes can make the process more expensive or harder than necessary and can dishearten a family or individual so that they give up the task completely.

1. Don't purchase storage items before you declutter the area. Many people buy shelves, bins, and boxes without understanding what they have or what they want to do with their stuff. After they get rid of items or come up with a plan for storing things, they realize that they don't have the right tools for the job. This results in an extra trip to the store which wastes both time and money. Instead, follow the steps for decluttering provided in this eBook before you purchase any storage options.

2. Don't try to get everything done in a single day. Depending on the size of your home and how much clutter you have, organization could take several weeks. Break the job into a single room, closet, or area. You can complete a small room in several hours, giving yourself a sense of accomplishment and allowing a day or two of rest before you start another project. Just make sure you aren't simply moving clutter from one room to another, as that will create a perpetual cycle.

3. Don't move from an area before you are done. Some people work several areas at a time or move onto the living room when they aren't done with the kitchen pantry. Leaving the job undone results in items sitting for days, weeks or months, adding to the clutter. You will find things are harder

to find when you leave them half organized. Leaving items in an unfinished state also encourages you simply to move them to another area to get them out of the way. If you cannot complete an area in the time you have, then come back to that area next time you are working on decluttering.

4. Don't get discouraged if clutter appears again. Decluttering is a lifelong habit, not a one-and-done job. Clutter comes from living in your space, and you can't stop yourself or your family from moving things, using things, or leaving things about. What you can do is develop habits of putting things away properly and using ten-minute cleaning sessions each day to reinforce organization and keep clutter at bay.

5. Don't chase after perfection. Attempting to keep your home in perfect shape, especially if you have children or pets, can be an overwhelming task and can cause extra stress or unhappiness with your area. Instead, realize that it is okay to live in your home and that there will almost always be something out of place. Being organized does not mean everything is always put away, but that you minimize the amount of items lying about, and everything has a place.

Reducing Clutter

In order to organize your stuff, you first need to determine what stuff is worth keeping. In this section, I provide a step-by-step plan for evaluating and handling your items. Instead of applying these steps to your whole house, use the plan to tackle a single room or area. For example, you could start with the linen closet, a bedroom closet, the attic, or the corner of the living room behind the couch. This will help you accomplish the task without getting overwhelmed. Once you have one area done, it is easy to apply these steps to the next area, and before you know it, you will have your house decluttered and under control.

Classify everything.

The first step in fighting clutter is labeling. You don't have to physically label each item, but you should assign every piece to a pile. Piles should be titled "Throw away," "Give away," "Repurpose," "Common Use," "Periodic Use," and "Décor/Keepsake." Each pile is described below.

- o Throw away
  Items in this pile are broken, outdated, or otherwise useless for any purpose. They also have no memorable or decorative value and should be thrown away or recycled.
- o Give away
  These are items you have no further use for but are still useful. Kids clothing is a great example of give-away items, especially if they were worn only once or twice. Give items to a friend or a charity. If you have time, you could also sell

items in a yard sale or on eBay to make money to fund storage item purchases.

- o Repurpose
  Some items are no longer useful as is, but may serve a different function within your home. Keep an eye out especially for items that can be turned into organizational or storage solutions such as old glass jars in the kitchen. Those can be repurposed to hold craft items, toiletries, and other items throughout the home.
- o Common use
  Common use items are those that are used daily or weekly. These items will need to be easy to reach and should be stored front and center in closets or on open shelves.
- o Periodic use
  Items that are used every few weeks or seasonally can be stored on higher shelves in closets or in attics, basements, or garages.
- o Keepsakes or décor items
  If you have keepsakes stuffed into a shelf or closet, consider using them as part of your home's décor. This reduces the cost of decoration and displays these items for all to see. You can use them on shelves or walls or create shadowboxes and other displays. Just make sure you don't go overboard and create additional clutter with your decorations. A good rule of thumb is to limit each foot of shelf space to one item or less.

Take Action

Once you create your piles, don't let them sit. Take action as soon as possible. That means carting things out to the curb, arranging donations and drop offs, storing items for resale, and putting things away in an appropriate manner. Create a single spot in your home for gathering items for a yard sale or future projects. This might be a corner in your garage or a spare room. Try to keep everything as organized as possible when you do this so you aren't simply creating another room of clutter to go through.

Use Frugal Organization Tips to Design a New Space

Once you have removed useless or unwanted items and understand how you want to use the items that you kept, you can begin organizing your space. You can either complete organizational steps for each room or you can spend a few days decluttering your entire house and then make one trip to purchase organizational supplies using the tips provided below.

Either way, make sure you have a plan in place before buying organizational supplies so that you reduce wasted time and money.

Organizing in a Frugal Fashion

You can save a lot of money by repurposing items in your home, shopping discount and dollar stores, and thinking outside of the box when it comes to organization.

A book shelf doesn't always have to be a book shelf, and you can do a lot with things like locker crates. Here is a look at some top tips for organizing in a frugal fashion.

Shop Dollar Stores for Storage Bargains

You can find many storage solutions at dollar stores, but you have to know what you are looking for. Sometimes dollars stores are places where everything costs one dollar or less, and other times, they are more like traditional Five and Dime stores.

Generally, you should avoid small shelves at these stores that require you to put them together, especially if you want to put heavier items on them. You can get a lot for a dollar, but there is a limit to the quality. Here is a list of things you can look for at the dollar store and what you might use them for:

- Mesh bags for storing and hauling dirty laundry also make great solutions for extra fabric or yarn in the craft room or storing stuffed animals in the kid's bedroom or playroom.
- Plastic under-bed storage bags can be used for clothing, blankets, soft toys, fabric, yarn, wrapping paper, and more.
- Plastic buckets and bins have unlimited uses: you can create colorful storage solutions on any shelf, organize small dry goods in the food pantry, sort toiletries in the bathroom, and store pens, markers, and other items in the home office.
- Cardboard file boxes can help you organize paperwork, photographs, toys, and kitchen items.
- Plastic crates of all sizes can be used as storage bins on shelves or turned sideways and stacked to make inexpensive shelving for CDs, DVDs, or lightweight toys.
- You can create attractive displays of art or photographs on the wall with a few nails, ribbon and clothes pins.
- Plastic food containers and zipper-seal storage bags are great for use in the kitchen or anywhere that small items need to be organized and stacked.
- Dollar stores also offer various wall racks and hooks for clothing, hats, and belts, as well as jars, cups, baskets, and other items that can be used for attractive and easy storage.

Shop Outside the Storage Aisle

You can often find an item that will do the same job at a lower cost by shopping outside of the storage aisle in your department store. There is something about the aisle labeled "Closet and Storage" that tends to inflate prices. A small shelf in this area could run you $30 when a similar shelf in the home improvement or DYI area is priced at $15. The difference is usually in finish, as the home décor sections will provide items that are sleek or meant to fit into certain décor styles. As long as you are willing to think outside of the box, however, you can save a ton of money.

One couple wanted a three foot by two-foot shelf to hold CDs. They needed the shelf to sit on top of a black and white cabinet in their living area. Browsing online and in stores like Ikea, they found the perfect shelf. It would hold over 120 CDs, had the right dimensions, and was solid black to match the cabinet. The shelf cost $130, though, and the couple didn't want to pay that much. It was August, and the couple visited Wal-Mart to do some school supply shopping for their son. While there, they found stackable locker crates that were the exact size for housing a dozen CDs. The crates were made of heavy-duty plastic, available in black, and were priced at $1.49 each. The couple purchased 14 crates and created their own shelf for $21. The crates provide a bit of modern industrial style and house all of the CDs perfectly. Even better, the couple can add on to the shelf anytime they want. Ultimately, this frugal shopping ended up saving them $119 plus shipping.

Shop other areas of any store you are in, looking for items that are on sale. Never limit the functionality of an item to the purpose for which it is being marketed. A mother needed a hat/scarf/belt rack for her pre-teen son. They lived in an A-frame house, so most walls were slanted. She wanted something that would mount on the back of his door, but was having a hard time finding something that would work in their space and was cost-effective. In the section of a department store that offered things like shower rods, she found an over-door hanger meant to hold five towels. The hooks were perfect for hanging hats and other clothing items and the rack hung over her son's door without any screws or nails.

Shop Used and Online

You can find some of the best deals in thrift stores, online, and at yard sales. Again, you need to be able to think outside of the box in order to make the best use of such shopping opportunities.

If you need somewhere to store your book collection, don't limit yourself to things that are obviously traditional bookcases. A college-aged man wanted to add bookshelves to one wall of his small apartment. He found wooden produce crates at a local thrift store. He decorated them with some paint, secured them together with screws, and created one-of-a-kind floor-to-ceiling shelving for less than $60. Plus, he repurposed these items, which meant they did not end up at a local landfill.

Look for crates, shelves of any kind, bins, baskets, bags, and anything else you can store items in. Don't let storage shopping add to your clutter, though. No matter how cute a particular item is, don't buy it if you can't think of a specific place in your home and organizational purpose for the piece.

Some areas to look for bargains or parts for these types of projects include Goodwill, Salvation Army Thrift Stores, Habitat for Humanity ReStores, Craigslist, eBay, and yard sales. If you shop online, make sure to follow common sense rules about meeting in a local, public place to exchange money for larger items. If you buy items to be shipped, make sure the seller provides plenty of pictures and that you pay via PayPal for buyer protection.

Use What You Already Have

If you can repurpose the items from a yard sale or store, you can do the same with items already in your home. An older couple inherited several items of furniture from a deceased aunt. One was a traditional kitchen buffet for which the couple didn't have a specific use. They did, however, want a nice piece of furniture to hold audio equipment in their dining room. They placed the buffet against a wall. Above, they hung a small flat screen television on the wall. The buffet included a wide top drawer, so they removed the front of the drawer, created a static bottom, and used hinges to turn the drawer front into a fall-down cabinet door. This created the perfect place for audio and video equipment, and the cabinets beneath that space offered storage for seasonal dishes.

When you are going through your items and creating declutter piles, question the organizational value of everything. This includes furniture, baskets, bins, jars, cups, racks, hooks, and more.

Organization for Your Entire Home: Decluttering Five Main Areas

Although the same basic rules apply throughout your home, each area comes with its own specific challenges. This section covers some specific organizational, declutter, and savings tips for five main areas of your home: Kitchen, living area, bedrooms, bathroom, and home office.

Tips for Decluttering the Kitchen

- To get the most out of pantry or refrigerator space, make use of rectangular, airtight plastic or glass food containers that can be stacked. These will prolong the life of your food, help you see in a few seconds what food you have available, and use more of the total storage space than round containers will.
- Create additional shelving in cabinets for canned goods and dry food items by stacking bins on their side. Store canned goods in rows of the same type of food with the oldest dates in front to avoid wasting food that is past the expiration date.
- Pick a day of each week to be "oldest food" day. Use the items that are nearest expiration date to make a meal. You can enter the items at Supercook.com to get suggested recipes for those ingredients you are trying to use.
- Adjust shelves in your refrigerator if possible to best accommodate your food storage needs. You might create taller spaces for juice and milk and shorter spaces for leftover food. Make sure you store leftovers toward the front where people can see them and never leave them in the fridge for more than four days in order to avoid building up unnecessary clutter.
- Use every space creatively, especially if you have a smaller kitchen. Small counter-top shelf or bin units can add storage space and protect the amount of work room you have. Hanging pots from ceiling racks (like the picture of the lovely copper pots in this section) or under cabinets keeps things organized. It can also add a decorative touch to your space without having to purchase additional decorations, which saves money.
- Install small hooks and racks on the inside door of cabinets to store smaller cookware or specialty utensils.
- Store appliances that are used less than once a week in lower or higher cabinets. If you use the item less than once a month, consider getting rid of it or storing it outside of the kitchen in a closet or basement.

Tips for Decluttering the Living room

- o Avoid the allure of coffee table books or magazines. Keep your coffee table free of any items or use only a single, striking decorative piece (see the example in the picture above). This offers a functional space for food or work items when you are using the space and provides a clutter-free, clean look at other times.
- o If you like to have books or magazines handy, purchase end or coffee tables with a secondary shelf or make use of a pretty basket or literature rack. Make sure you put away books after you are done reading them and throw outdated magazines out in order to avoid building clutter in your literature rack.
- o Purchase a pretty bin, basket, or tray to house all remote controls for home entertainment systems. Place this item in an easy to reach place such as a shelf under the coffee table

or on a side table nearby the main seating area. Placing small, regularly used items in a container reduces the look of clutter and also makes it easier to clean. When dusting a table, it is much easier to pick up a single basket than to move four or five remote controls.

- ○ Find easy-to-carry, sizeable bins for the entire family. Fabric bins work well for this purpose and can be color coordinated to your room. You can also purchase inexpensive plastic bins at the dollar store. Mark each bin with a person's name by having them embroidered or using colorful permanent marker. Keep these bins in a discreet or out of the way location in your living area. As you move through the area during the day, pick up articles of clothing, books, toys, and other stray items and put them in the appropriate bin. At the end of the day, everyone can pick up his or her bin and put the items away, helping to fight clutter in only a few minutes. This way everybody has a job, and the task of keeping clutter at bay does not fall on one household member.
- ○ Avoid overstuffing your coat closet by getting rid of items that haven't been worn in the past two months. This doesn't mean throwing things out, as you'll probably need the winter clothing at some point. However, if you aren't going to wear an article of clothing soon, box it up and store it under a bed, in an attic, or on a high shelf in a closet.
- ○ If you have a shelf at the top of the coat closet, place bins or baskets on it labeled "hats," "gloves," and "scarves." If you live in a warmer client, you might have baskets labeled "beach towels," "goggles," and "pool toys." Choose items that you use often and organize them in such a way that makes them easy to locate.
- ○ If your family uses blankets or afghans on a regular basis while watching movies or television, consider purchasing a block ottoman that offers storage space under the cushion. This is the perfect place for stashing a few blanks, but you could also use the area for extra media, books, or even

family board games. The ottoman then offers functionality for putting up your feet or extra seating when you are entertaining a large number of guests.

Tips for Decluttering Bedrooms

- o Make use of all the space within your room, but avoid filling it all with clutter. You can use the space under your bed by purchasing inexpensive boxes or plastic containers made to store things beneath the mattress. This is a perfect place to store extra bedding or out-of-season clothing, because it is cool and dry. Storing items under the bed in zippered bags or sealed containers also lengthens the life of clothing and other fabric, which can save money over time.
- o In kid's bedrooms, use under-bed storage bins to house LEGOs, blocks, trains, Barbies and other toys that come with

lots of parts. Kids can pull these bins out when they want and slide them back under the bed when playtime is over.

- o Take photos of the kids' toys so you can label the boxes/containers for them to put their things away. Label other containers with what goes in there (example: gloves & winter hats).
- o Make sure dressers and other drawers are being used to the best benefit. If only three pair of jeans will fit in the drawer, you are better off hanging those in the closet and using the drawer for neatly folded shirts or smaller items. Some people simply stuff items into the drawer, but you will save space and locate your items faster if you put them away folded and in an orderly fashion. That is true even for things like socks or undergarments.
- o Use the back of doors and wall space where possible for organization. You can purchase plastic hanging sets from the dollar or discount store that will convert the back of a bedroom or closet door into a shoe rack, jewelry holder, or accessory storage area.

- Ladies should choose a single location for cosmetics. Make sure it has suitable lighting, a mirror, and a way to organize makeup and other items. Keep everything in the same place for convenience.
- Make the beds every day. Simply making the bed creates and orderly look in the room and will encourage you to put things away instead of leaving them on the bed, dresser, or tables.
- Avoid keeping exercise equipment in the bedroom if possible, since such items tend to attract clutter and clothing.
- A small table or nightstand next to each occupied side of the bed is great for housing an alarm clock, lamp, and a book or other item. However, avoid allowing items to pile up. If you don't use the item every evening, then remove it from the bedside table. Place a small basket on the table for loose items like eye glasses, lip balm, telephones, and other things that you might want to keep handy during the night.
- Only keep clothing hanging in your closet that you will wear in the next two to three months. All other items can be thrown away, given away, sold, or put away for another season.
- Fold sweaters and keep them on shelves in the closet to reduce clutter or bulk in your dresser.
- Try to keep closets functional where possible. This means that seasonal items and decorations should be stored in attics, basements, and garages. If you must use closet space for such items, put them at the highest or lowest locations, since you will not need to access them often.
- Store specialty dress shoes in their boxes, but keep shoes you wear on a weekly or biweekly basis in a shoe rack, shelving, or over-the-door hanger.

Tips for Decluttering the Bathroom

- o Some people like to add a lot of décor to their bathroom. Instead of many small items that will collect dust and germs, choose a few items that convey your sense of style. This is especially effective if the items double as functional elements. For example, you could decorate a small bathroom with a nice color of wall paint and a striking shower curtain. Other elements that could add a touch of style include soap dispensers, toothbrush holders, and towel racks. Avoid hard-to-clean décor elements such as faux flowers or greenery.
- o Keep small items organized in bathroom drawers or on shelves by using bins and baskets. This is where you can go wild in the dollar store to create attractive storage sets for cosmetics, sanitary items, shampoos, conditioners, and more.
- o Make sure you can see what you have. Many people toss extra bottles of shampoo or bars of soap under the

bathroom sink and forget about them. Then, they keep buying and storing the same items, wasting a lot of money and adding to the bathroom clutter. Place a bin under the sink and set these items in an orderly fashion. You should be able to look under the sink and count how many of each item you have in just a few seconds.

- You don't need to keep one of everything in the shower, especially if everyone in the house uses a different shampoo, soap, body wash, or conditioner. Instead, purchase a small plastic caddy for each person and store them on a convenient shelf. All personal bath and shower items can be stored in that caddy, which is pulled out when each person takes a shower. Only keep items in the shower that everyone uses on a regular basis.
- Consider dividing bathroom storage areas to allow each individual a personal space. If there aren't enough drawers in the bathroom cabinetry, separate shelving with different colored bins. Ask each person to go through his or her bin once a week to organize it and get rid of unnecessary items like empty bottles.

Tips for Decluttering the Home Office

If your home office looks like the one in the picture above, it is obviously time to declutter. A space that looks like that is not usable and only adds to the stress of dealing with household finances and other home office chores.

o   You can use many of the storage tips for other rooms in the home office, including stacking plastic bins on their sides to create inexpensive shelving.

o   Don't bring junk mail in house have a basket or trash container right where you bring the mail in so you can throw it away. Immediately put important bills in an in box that you take care of on a weekly basis.

o   Consider peg boards on the wall to house supplies like scissors, pens, markers, packs of crayons and colored pencils, scotch tape, and rulers. These are things everyone in the home uses on a regular basis, and housing them in an easy to see location makes it easy to know when you are running low on an essential tool.

- o Keep cables and cords together. It is easy for these to become a jumbled mess, and then you lose track of important cords and cables. User plastic ties to help keep them together, or purchase special cord storage units that you clearly label with the cord or cable's use.
- o Use a flat table instead of a traditional computer desk for a clean look in the room. You may be surprised how little you really need drawers in desk when you no longer have them. In most cases, drawers are simply an invitation to stuff things away and often create more clutter than they are worth.
- o Invest in a good scanner and software to reduce the clutter associated with paperwork and file cabinets. Your investment will pay off by reducing the time it takes you to find important paperwork. A well-organized digital filing system can also increase your savings when it comes to tax returns, rebates, and coupon shopping.
- o Sometimes you really do need to keep the original, but you might not have time to file everything the second it arrives. Instead of tossing it on the desk, buy a small magazine holder or inbox and place it in a convenient location. Put items that need to be filed in that box and take fifteen minutes each week to file those items.
- o Invest in a paper shredder. That way you can safely dispose of items that it is time to throw away that contain sensitive financial or personal information. It is easy to let these items pile up if you do not own a shredder.
- o Many times, people forget to dust and clean their home office when they do the rest of the house. Computers and electronics attract a lot of dust, so make sure you wipe tables and other areas in your office on a regular basis to keep it clean.

Declutter as a Family

Make sure that you get the whole household involved in organizing and fighting clutter. Even small toddlers can learn to put their toys away when they are done. In fact, small children will probably come to appreciate this practice, as they will be able to find toys when they want them and may discover long-lost toys they had forgotten about.

Trying to keep an entire home decluttered on your own is a great way to fight a losing battle, so make sure everyone understands the importance of the endeavor and agrees to do his or her part of the decluttering. This helps make sure that decluttering becomes a way of life for your household, and it will mean much less time spent decluttering for you. In addition, it will teach the younger members of your household good organizational skills that will last a lifetime.

- Make sure each family member has a "decluttering" responsibility. This will not only help keep the house straight, but it will also give young children responsibility and a sense of accomplishment for taking care of his or her job.
- Set aside time in the family's daily or weekly schedule specifically devoted to picking up clutter that is laying around after the day's activities are over. If you have young children in the household, routines are very likely everything, so just build this into your regular routine, and it will not feel like a chore for anybody. It will just be a regular part of the household's day or week.

Decluttering Childrens' Incoming Paper

Be sure to keep a handle on what comes into the house with kids. If they attend school or daycare, the chances are, they will bring home dozens of papers each day. Obviously all of these cannot be saved.

- o Look through all the papers your child brings home. Sort them based on what must be taken care of like notes, what is their work, and what is artwork
- o Take care of items like notes and other important things that require action, and then recycle them.
- o Prepare to keep a lot of your children's' artwork in the short-term. Choose a place in the home to display their most recently art, and change that out on a weekly or daily basis. Create a memory box to save the most special pieces of artwork your children bring home.
- o Look through your children's' schoolwork. Discard the typical worksheets and other work that comes home. If it is something special like a story your child has written, consider putting it in the memory box with other special artwork. If it is an especially good grade that your child is proud of, display it in the household.

Conclusion: Anyone Can Live Clutter-Free

People make a lot of excuses for their clutter. They don't have time to deal with the mess, organization is expensive, or their home is too small. The truth is that anyone can live clutter-free, regardless of space or budget constraints. The keys to decluttering your life and living in a reduced-stress, beautiful environment are:

- Making a serious choice to take action.
- Following this proven approach to declutter.
- Thinking outside the box when it comes to organization.
- Making decluttering a lifestyle choice rather than a single cleaning activity.

The benefits to organizing each room in your home include cost and time savings. Many people also believe that an organized home that is free of clutter impacts mental and emotional health by making it easier to relax in your space, reducing stress associated with stuff, and allowing you to use your home the way it was designed.

This eBook covers some of the main areas of your home, but you can use the tips and tricks to organize your garage, basement, attic, professional workspace, children's playroom, and even your yard, pool house, or shed. Organizing and decluttering may sound like a lot of work, but once you get that first room completed, you will probably enjoy the benefits so much you are driven to complete other areas in your home. The amount of stress that falls off your shoulders when living in a clutter-free space is completely worth the time, effort, planning, and money involved in decluttering.

More Home & Health Resource Guides

Essential Oils Guide: Reference for Living Young, Healing, Weight Loss, Aromatherapy & Recipes

Healthy Eating Guide for Busy Women: Dieting & Weight Loss Tips

Busy Mom's Guide: Running for Fitness, Weight Loss & Health

Printed in Great Britain
by Amazon